ALL KINDS OF
PLANES

ALL KINDS OF PLANES

By Seymour Reit

Pictures by
Roberto Innocenti

Golden Press • New York

Western Publishing Company, Inc.
Racine, Wisconsin

Library of Congress Catalog Card Number: 78-50866

The first people to try to fly used homemade wings, but wing flapping was strictly for the birds!

A great thinker named Leonardo Da Vinci drew sketches for flying machines 500 years ago. He did this after he had studied how birds fly. He also had ideas for a parachute and a helicopter. But the machines he planned were never built.

A flying machine designed to look like this was thought of by a scientist around 1670.

A glider has no power of its own. It is carried by the wind. On breezeless days it can't fly at all.

This balloon was filled with a lighter-than-air gas called hydrogen. The flier tried to steer with a sail.

Early balloons were filled with heated air, which made them rise.

EARLY PLANES

People have always dreamed of being able to fly, but for many years no one knew how. Early experimenters built wings and tied them to their arms, hoping to fly like birds. Scientists drew sketches of flying machines and thought about "sky boats" steered by "air paddles." But only about 200 years ago did people begin to fly at last. The first fliers went up in balloons and in giant kites called gliders.

Count slowly: 1...2...3...
4...5...6...7...8...9...10...
11...12. That is how long the
first airplane flight lasted—
just 12 seconds!

That first flight took place in
1903, in America. The fliers, Wilbur and Orville Wright,
were brothers. They were the first ones ever to fly and
control a powered flying machine. And on that day in 1903,
they changed the future of the world.

the Wright brothers

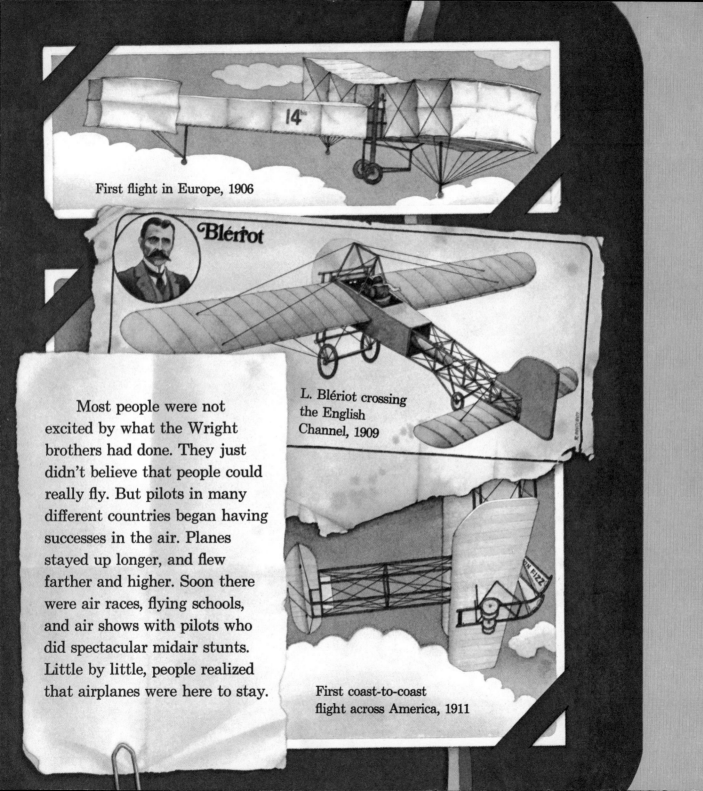

First flight in Europe, 1906

Blériot

L. Blériot crossing
the English
Channel, 1909

Most people were not
excited by what the Wright
brothers had done. They just
didn't believe that people could
really fly. But pilots in many
different countries began having
successes in the air. Planes
stayed up longer, and flew
farther and higher. Soon there
were air races, flying schools,
and air shows with pilots who
did spectacular midair stunts.
Little by little, people realized
that airplanes were here to stay.

First coast-to-coast
flight across America, 1911

When the airplane was still a very new invention and most people thought it was only good for circus stunts, a great World War broke out. The airplane's first practical job was as a weapon. It was used for spying and fighting, while airships called dirigibles were sometimes used for bombing. Many pilots became war heroes.

After the war, pilots continued to do brave deeds. One of the most famous pilots ever was Charles Lindbergh. He flew across the vast Atlantic Ocean—by himself! No one had ever done that before. He flew 3,600 miles. It took nearly 34 hours. When he arrived in France, a huge crowd of people carried him on their shoulders. "Lucky Lindy" was a hero.

Amelia Earhart was another famous pilot. She became known for her daring long-distance flights.

Caproni
(Italy)

Spad (France)

Sopwith Camel
(Great Britain)

Amazed fishermen spied Lindbergh's plane as he flew across the Atlantic. Most of them had never seen an airplane before.

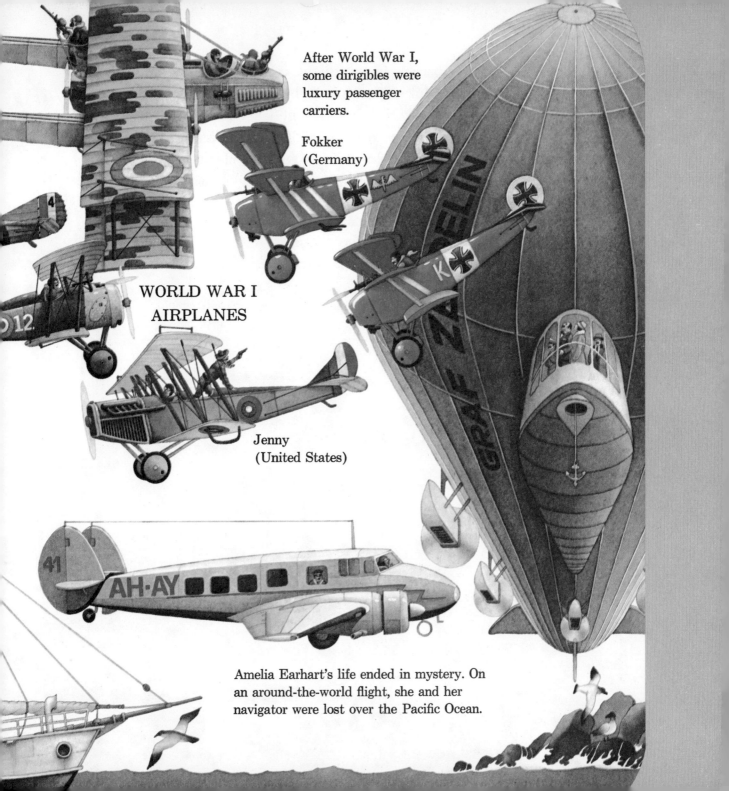

After World War I, some dirigibles were luxury passenger carriers.

Fokker (Germany)

WORLD WAR I AIRPLANES

Jenny (United States)

Amelia Earhart's life ended in mystery. On an around-the-world flight, she and her navigator were lost over the Pacific Ocean.

After Lindbergh's famous flight, changes came fast. More powerful airplanes were built, and longer flights were possible. Now planes were made of metal, instead of wood and cloth. More and more airplanes were used to carry freight and mail. Special planes just for passengers were built. People began to visit parts of the world they hadn't been able to reach before. Airplanes made the world seem smaller.

Zero
(Japan)

With this plane, passengers traveled quickly, safely, and comfortably for the first time.

Giant seaplanes carried passengers, freight, or mail across the oceans.

WORLD WAR II AIRPLANES

Zero (Japan)

Lightning
(United States)

Flying Fortress
(United States)

Spitfire
(Great Britain)

Stuka (Germany)

This rocket plane was the first aircraft
to fly faster than the speed of sound.

TODAY'S PLANES

A modern airport is a very busy place. Every few minutes, a plane takes off or lands. Now another flight is about to leave. The fuel tanks are filled, and the engines have been checked. Passengers and baggage are on board. The crew looks over the instruments.

When all is ready, the Captain taxis the plane to the runway, and waits. At last the control tower sends the message: "You are cleared for takeoff!" And another flight zooms on its way.

helicopter

Boeing 727

Douglas DC-10

Fokker F-27

Boeing 737

Boeing 707

Douglas DC-8

FLUGHAFEN

LOT

16

PARKING

Today there are many kinds of planes, and they do many different jobs. Some are "flying gas stations." They refuel smaller planes in midair. Others are cargo carriers. They take goods and products all over the world. Some of these sky freighters can haul more than 300,000 pounds. This equals the weight of 50 elephants!

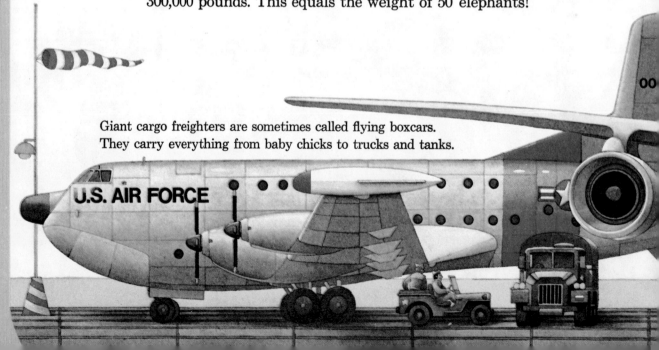

Giant cargo freighters are sometimes called flying boxcars. They carry everything from baby chicks to trucks and tanks.

U.S. AIR FORCE

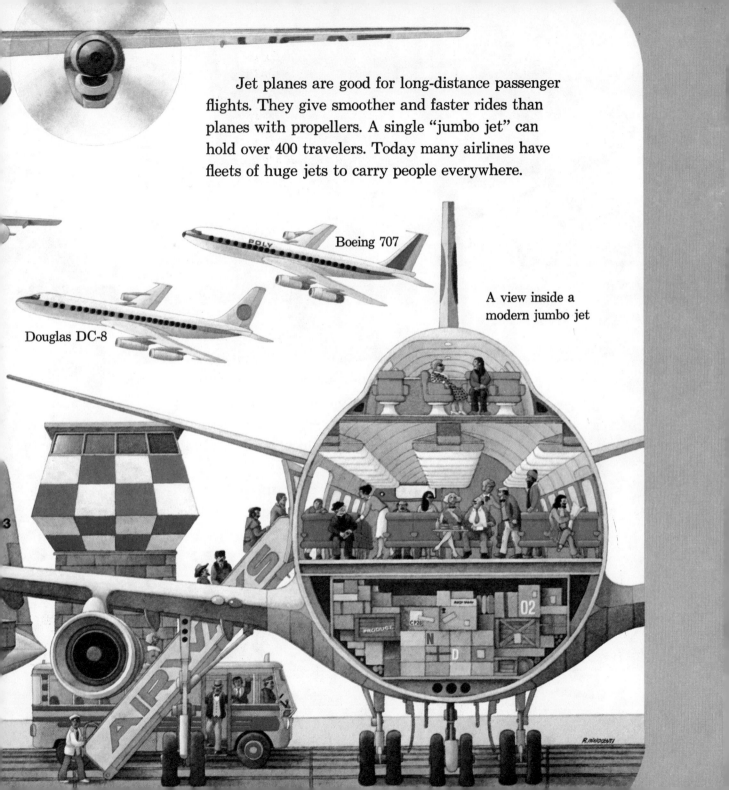

Jet planes are good for long-distance passenger flights. They give smoother and faster rides than planes with propellers. A single "jumbo jet" can hold over 400 travelers. Today many airlines have fleets of huge jets to carry people everywhere.

Boeing 707

Douglas DC-8

A view inside a modern jumbo jet

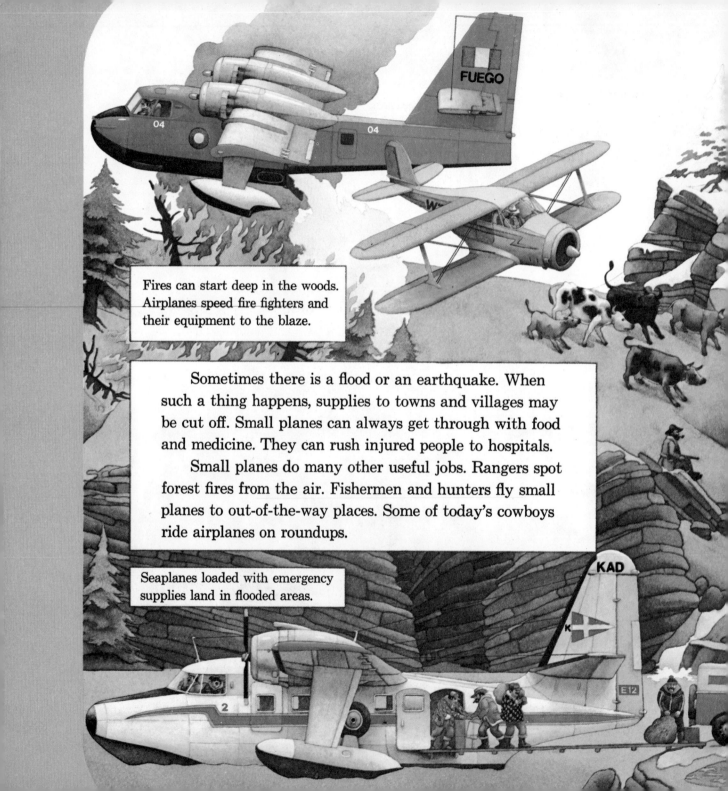

Fires can start deep in the woods. Airplanes speed fire fighters and their equipment to the blaze.

Sometimes there is a flood or an earthquake. When such a thing happens, supplies to towns and villages may be cut off. Small planes can always get through with food and medicine. They can rush injured people to hospitals.

Small planes do many other useful jobs. Rangers spot forest fires from the air. Fishermen and hunters fly small planes to out-of-the-way places. Some of today's cowboys ride airplanes on roundups.

Seaplanes loaded with emergency supplies land in flooded areas.

Rescue planes search for people lost on mountains.

Farmers use small planes to spray their crops against diseases. In Canada and other places where snowfalls are very heavy, planes drop bales of hay to hungry animals. Where homes and ranches are far apart, doctors and veterinarians may make house calls in small planes.

"Crop duster" planes can spray large fields quickly.

Some doctors' planes are like hospitals on wings.

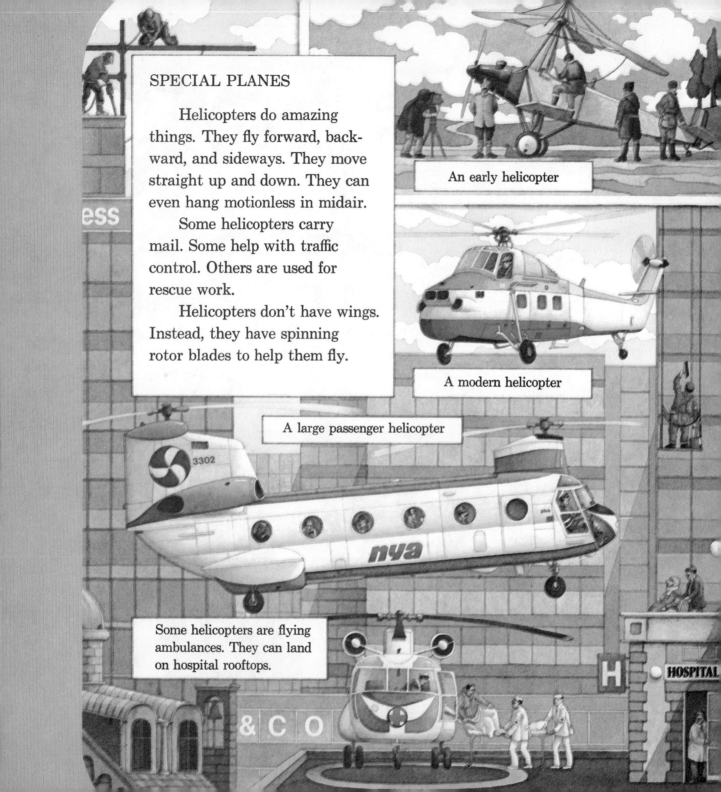

SPECIAL PLANES

Helicopters do amazing things. They fly forward, backward, and sideways. They move straight up and down. They can even hang motionless in midair.

Some helicopters carry mail. Some help with traffic control. Others are used for rescue work.

Helicopters don't have wings. Instead, they have spinning rotor blades to help them fly.

An early helicopter

A modern helicopter

A large passenger helicopter

Some helicopters are flying ambulances. They can land on hospital rooftops.

HOSPITAL

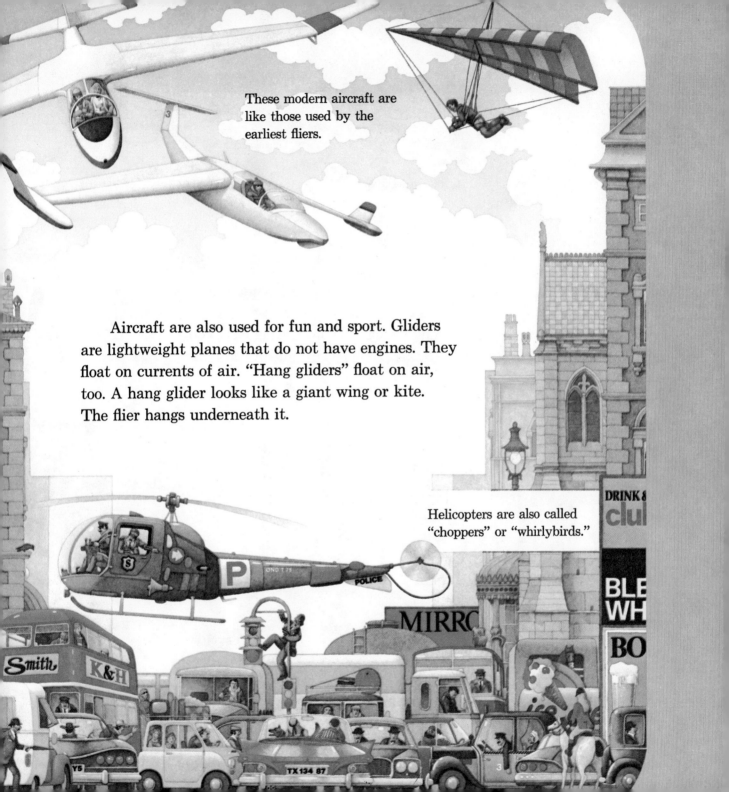

These modern aircraft are like those used by the earliest fliers.

Aircraft are also used for fun and sport. Gliders are lightweight planes that do not have engines. They float on currents of air. "Hang gliders" float on air, too. A hang glider looks like a giant wing or kite. The flier hangs underneath it.

Helicopters are also called "choppers" or "whirlybirds."

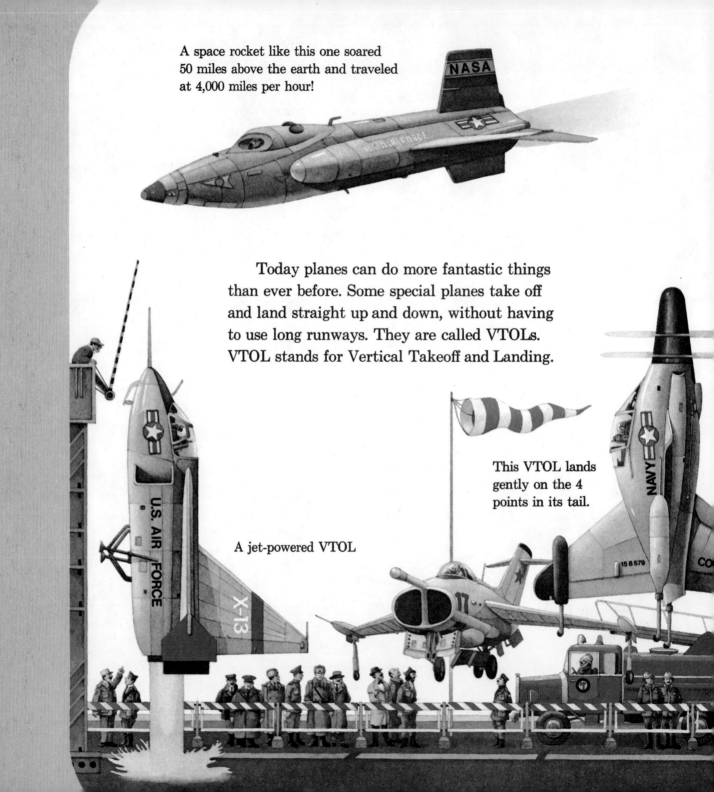

A space rocket like this one soared
50 miles above the earth and traveled
at 4,000 miles per hour!

Today planes can do more fantastic things
than ever before. Some special planes take off
and land straight up and down, without having
to use long runways. They are called VTOLs.
VTOL stands for Vertical Takeoff and Landing.

This VTOL lands
gently on the 4
points in its tail.

A jet-powered VTOL

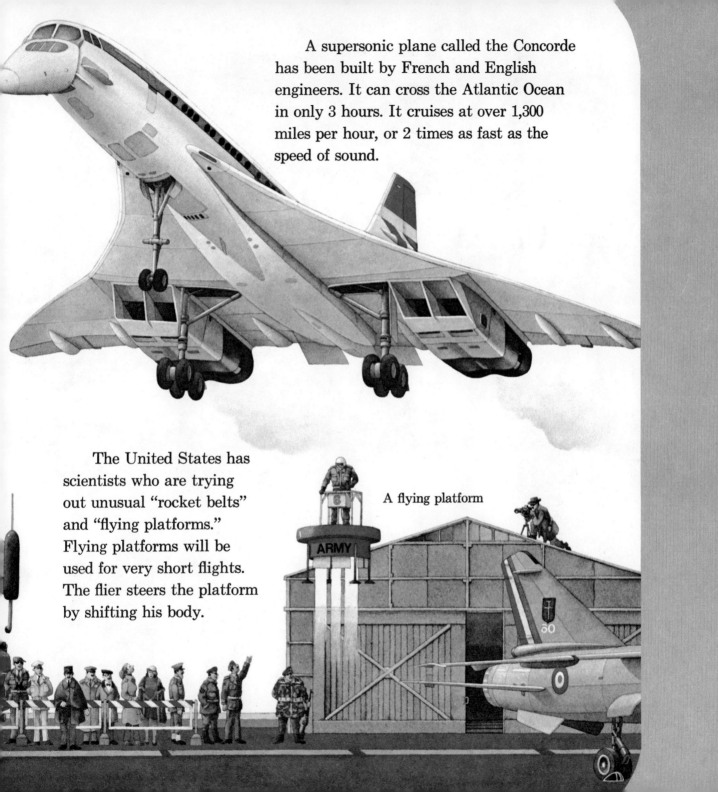

A supersonic plane called the Concorde has been built by French and English engineers. It can cross the Atlantic Ocean in only 3 hours. It cruises at over 1,300 miles per hour, or 2 times as fast as the speed of sound.

The United States has scientists who are trying out unusual "rocket belts" and "flying platforms." Flying platforms will be used for very short flights. The flier steers the platform by shifting his body.

A flying platform

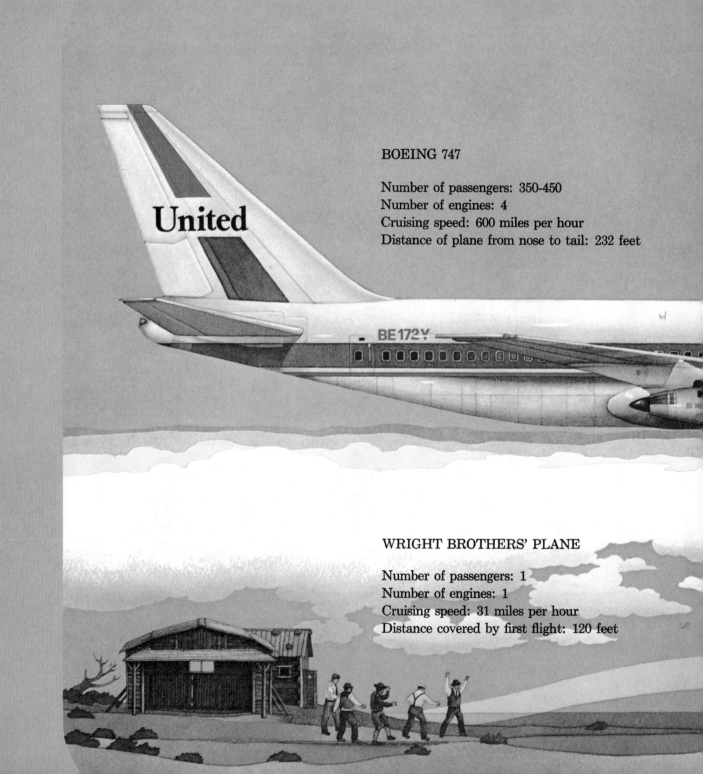

BOEING 747

Number of passengers: 350-450
Number of engines: 4
Cruising speed: 600 miles per hour
Distance of plane from nose to tail: 232 feet

WRIGHT BROTHERS' PLANE

Number of passengers: 1
Number of engines: 1
Cruising speed: 31 miles per hour
Distance covered by first flight: 120 feet

WE'VE COME A LONG WAY

Look up at the sky. Wait a moment or two, and chances are you'll see an airplane fly by. Right this minute, there are hundreds of planes flying to places all over the world.

Since the Wright brothers, there have been many wondrous changes in air travel—changes that have come very fast. Here's a fact that sums it all up: From its nose to its tail, the modern jumbo jet is much longer than the entire distance covered by the Wright brothers in their first flight in 1903!